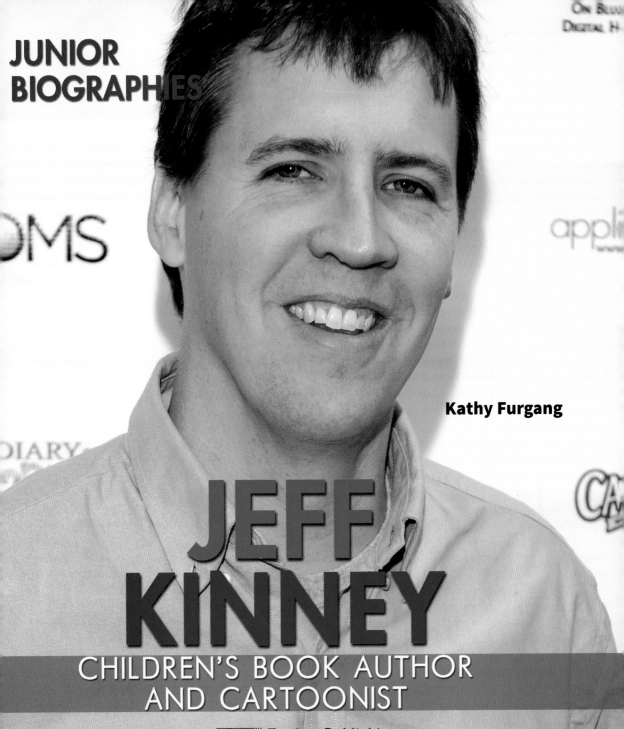

JUNIOR
BIOGRAPHIES

Kathy Furgang

JEFF KINNEY
CHILDREN'S BOOK AUTHOR
AND CARTOONIST

Enslow Publishing
101 W. 23rd Street
Suite 240
New York, NY 10011
USA

enslow.com

WORDS TO KNOW

fantasy A kind of writing that uses magic and adventure, often set in another world.

graduate To finish a school.

influential Having a great effect on others.

journal A personal record of thoughts, events, and feelings, similar to a diary.

publish To print something so it is available to many.

rehash To retell or reexperience something.

sibling A brother or sister.

CONTENTS

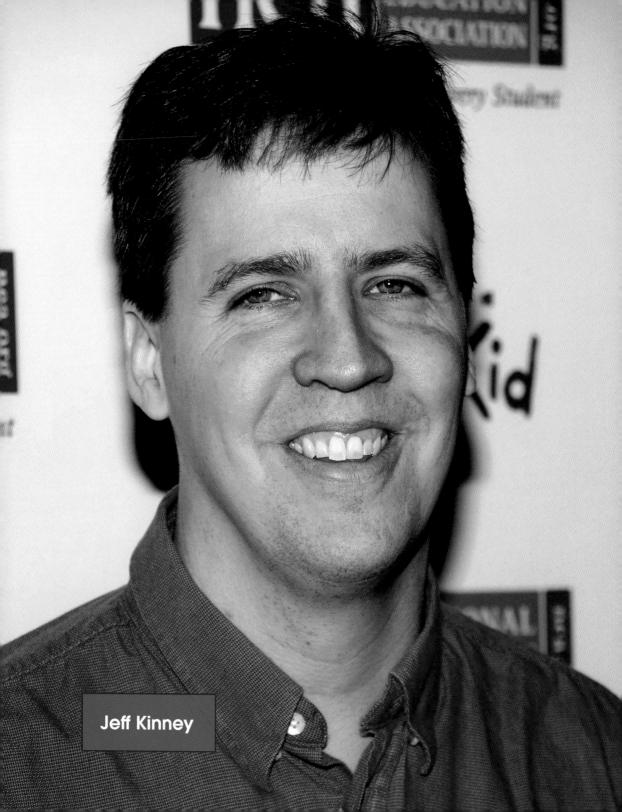

Jeff Kinney

CHAPTER 1

A YOUNG JEFF KINNEY

What makes someone a great children's author? As Jeff Kinney knows, it's getting kids to love reading. This best-selling author has definitely done that! Millions of kids around the world have read Jeff's Diary of a Wimpy Kid book series.

Jeff Kinney was born on an air force base in Maryland on February 19, 1971. His father worked for the government and his mother was a teacher. As a young boy, Jeff loved reading. His childhood home was filled with many books. He and his sister enjoyed reading books by Judy Blume and Beverly Cleary. As he got older, Jeff enjoyed reading **fantasy** books. But what he really loved was reading from his father's comic book collection.

Jeff went to the University of Maryland, where he studied computer science and drew cartoons for the school newspaper.

A LOVE OF ART

When Jeff **graduated** high school, he went to the University of Maryland at College Park. While he was there, he found that he loved drawing comic books. He drew a comic strip called *Igdoof* for his school newspaper. Igdoof was awkward and hated school (much like the main character of the Wimpy Kid books). The cartoon was very

Jeff Says:

"I think if everyone would write down the funny stories from their own childhoods, the world would be a better place."

popular. Jeff hoped that he could continue the comic strip after he left school.

A NEW COMIC

Even though he tried hard, Jeff could not reach his dream. He was not able to get a newspaper to **publish** *Igdoof.* But he did not give up. In 1998, Jeff started collecting ideas for a new comic, *Diary of a Wimpy Kid.* The stories were about a middle schooler named Greg Heffley, his family, and his best friend, Rowley. Jeff did not know it at the time, but the comic would one day become a best-selling book series.

Jeff's fifth grade teacher, Mrs. Norton, encouraged her students to try to be funny and go for the best jokes possible. She also told Jeff to plan his drawings ahead of time, and to "think before you ink."

Chapter 2
A Wimpy Kid Is Born

Jeff's Wimpy Kid idea was not an overnight success. He worked hard on it for six years before he began publishing it online at funbrain.com. Each day of the character's journal entries could be read online, day by day. (People can still read the comics online today.)

Finally, in 2006, a publisher decided to turn Jeff's comic strips into a printed book. *Diary of a Wimpy Kid* was published in 2007. Kids easily understood the main character, Greg, and his adventures as a student who was

Jeff turns in around eight drafts of each of his books. Each book contains about 350 drawings, and each takes about an hour for Jeff to finish.

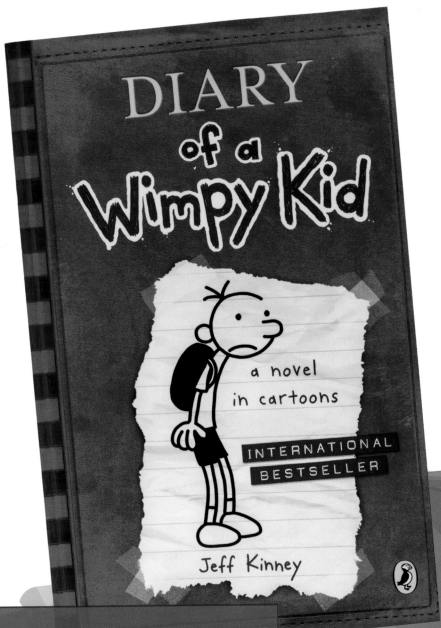

The cover of Jeff's first Wimpy Kid book. It took many years for his comics to become a book.

Jeff uses a computer as he creates new art for a Wimpy Kid book.

new to middle school. The line drawings made the stories feel fun and comic. The handwritten text made the book feel like actual journal entries of Greg's feelings and experiences.

WORLD FAMOUS

Diary of a Wimpy Kid was a huge success. The best-selling book was proof that people wanted to read more about Greg Heffley and his adventures in middle school. The following year, in 2008, the second book in the series, *Rodrick Rules*, was released.

THE SERIES GROWS

Jeff continued to write more books for the popular new series. By 2017, he was working on the twelfth book,

Jeff Says:
"To come out and meet kids who have my books in their hands is kind of amazing."

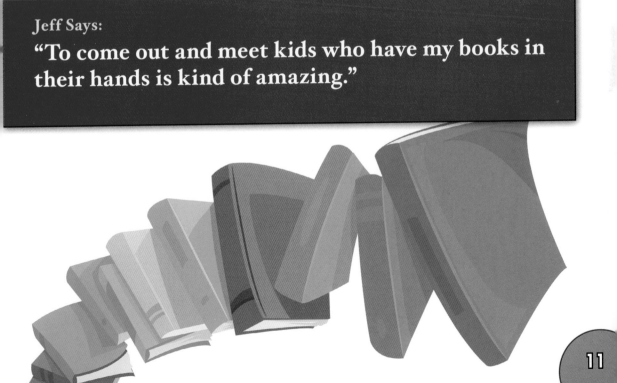

A scene from the 2010 movie *Diary of a Wimpy Kid*, starring (*left to right*) Robert Capron, Zachary Gordon, and Chloë Moretz.

called *The Getaway*. He also wrote two extra books related to the series. In 2010, the series was turned into a full-length film. Since then, more movies have been made and they have all been successful with young people.

CHAPTER 3

IT'S ALL ABOUT THE STORY

Ever since Jeff was a child, storytelling was important to him. He remembers that his grandmother used to tell his family the same stories over and over again. "We would always enjoy the stories as if we were hearing them for the first time. And now, today, I still call my siblings and we rehash these old stories of things that happened to us as kids. I think that has really helped shape the Wimpy Kid books."

Jeff has fond memories of the old books that he read as a child. Keeping them has helped to make a kind of time capsule of his youth. He can still look back today at what he was interested in during different stages of his life.

POPTROPICA

Although the Wimpy Kid books are what made Jeff famous, that is not all he does. He's another kind of

Jeff works on a cartoon. In addition to his books, he is busy working on his website, Poptropica.

storyteller, too. Jeff is an online game developer and designer. He created an interactive website for kids called Poptropica.com. In the games, kids make a character and travel to islands having adventures. Sometimes they solve mysteries. Other times they learn about history. In

Jeff Says:

"I'm keeping my day job, because Poptropica is something that really energizes me."

Jeff attends an event with his two sons, Will and Grant.

their adventures, kids can read digital books or comics. They can watch movies or collect objects. They can even watch short movies in the games.

Over 180 million copies of Wimpy Kid books have been sold around the world.

Jeff enjoys doing this type of work as well as writing the Wimpy Kid books. Poptropica is for younger children than the Wimpy Kid books. He likes introducing the six-, seven-, and eight-year-olds to history through the interactive stories.

CANDY OR VITAMINS?

Jeff is good at telling stories for kids. But what about the stories behind the Wimpy Kid books? They are often about growing up and going through changes. More than

Kids line up to have Jeff sign their books.

anything else, however, Jeff wants kids to have fun reading the books. He sees the Wimpy Kid books more as a way to deliver jokes than to tell a complex story.

Jeff once said in an interview, "My books are candy and they don't have a lot of vitamins." Even though the books are fun, Jeff thinks kids should read all kinds of books. "I think that kids need their vitamins, too."

CHAPTER 4
DON'T BE A WIMP, READ!

Jeff has made a big difference for kids who don't like to read. His books make them laugh. In 2009, Jeff was named in *Time* magazine's list of the world's most influential people. At first, Jeff did not understand why he would receive such a high honor. But then he realized why his work was important: It turns kids on to reading.

INSPIRING GENERATIONS OF KIDS

Jeff Kinney will continue to inspire kids with Poptropica and the Wimpy Kid series. As kids get older, they will be able to introduce younger people to the books they love.

Jeff Says:

"My life is pretty ordinary in so many ways. I live in a town called Plainville. I have the life of an average dad. It feels like I have this secret identity as an author."

Children across the country love reading Jeff's books.

Jeff opened his own bookstore in his hometown of Plainville, Massachusetts.

When kids can learn to love reading as children, they will likely love it as adults, too.

Jeff lives in Plainville, Massachusetts, with his wife and two sons.

Jeff takes about nine months to write a Wimpy Kid book from start to finish. He starts with hundreds of image ideas and writes the story around them.

TIMELINE

1971 Jeff Kinney is born on February 19, 1971, in Maryland.

1990 Begins attending University of Maryland.

1995 Moves from Maryland to New England.

1998 Starts working on his Wimpy Kid comic strip.

2004 Turns Wimpy Kid into a daily journal at funbrain .com.

2007 Starts his website Poptropica.

2007 *Diary of a Wimpy Kid* is published as Jeff's first book.

2009 Jeff is named one of *Time* magazine's most influential people.

2010 The first Wimpy Kid movie is released.

2012 Wins Author of the Year at the Children's Choice Book Awards.

2015 Jeff and his wife open their own bookstore, called An Unlikely Story, in Plainville, Massachusetts.

LEARN MORE

BOOKS

Hicks, Kelli L., and Michael Byers. *Jeff Kinney*. Mankato, MN: Capstone Press, 2013.

Kinney, Patrick, and John Hinderliter. *Who Is Jeff Kinney?* New York, NY: Grosset & Dunlap, 2015.

Leaf, Christina. *Jeff Kinney*. Hopkins, MN: Bellwether Media, 2016.

WEBSITES

Poptropica

www.poptropica.com

Play at the website that Jeff Kinney created—and explore interactive worlds and stories through games.

Wimpy Kid

www.wimpykid.com

Visit the *Diary of a Wimpy Kid* website to learn more about the books, movies, and author.

Funbrain

www.funbrain.com

Read the Wimpy Kid books the way they were originally published—on funbrain.com in daily journal entries.

INDEX

Published in 2018 by Enslow Publishing, LLC.
101 W. 23rd Street, Suite 240, New York, NY 10011

Library of Congress Cataloging-in-Publication Data
Names: Furgang, Kathy author.
Title: Jeff Kinney : children's book author and cartoonist / Kathy Furgang.
Description: New York, NY : Enslow Publishing, LLC, 2018. | Series: Junior
  biographies | Includes bibliographical references and index. | Audience: Grades 3-5.
Identifiers: LCCN 2017015428| ISBN 9780766090637 (library bound) | ISBN
  9780766090613 (pbk.) | ISBN 9780766090620 (6 pack)
Subjects: LCSH: Kinney, Jeff–Juvenile literature. | Authors, American–20th
  century–Biography–Juvenile literature. | Children's
  stories–Authorship–Juvenile literature. | Cartoonists–United
  States–Biography–Juvenile literature.
Classification: LCC PS3611.I634 Z55 2017 | DDC 813/.6 [B] –dc23
LC record available at https://lccn.loc.gov/2017015428

Printed in China

To Our Readers: We have done our best to make sure all website addresses in this book were active and appropriate when we went to press. However, the author and the publisher have no control over and assume no liability for the material available on those websites or on any websites they may link to. Any comments or suggestions can be sent by email to customerservice@enslow.com.

Photo Credits: Cover, p. 1 Mike Pont/Getty Images; p. 4 Bryan Bedder/Getty Images; p. 6 Loop Images/Universal Images Group/ Getty Images; p. 9 razorpix/Alamy Stock Photo; pp. 10, 14 Boston Globe/Getty Images; p. 12 Photo 12/Alamy Stock Photo; p. 15 Invision for Twentieth Century Fox Home Entertainment/AP; p. 17 © Napa Valley Register/ZUMAPRESS.com; p. 19 The Washington Post/Getty Images; p. 20 © AP Images; back cover, pp. 2, 3, 22, 23, 24 (curves graphic) Alena Kazlouskaya/Shutterstock. com; interior page bottoms (books) Lorelyn Medina/Shutterstock.com.